AF413391

ALPHA
Code of Influence

ALPHA
Code of Influence

50 Laws for Mastering Power Dynamics

Luciano Layne

ALPHA Magazines

Just a reminder from me to you...

You are stronger than you think. Keep pushing forward, and you will overcome any obstacle that comes your way. Remember, strength is not just physical, it's mental and emotional too. Stay resilient and never give up.
Your strength is like a shining light that inspires others. Keep shining, keep growing, and keep believing in yourself. You are capable of incredible things. You possess an inner strength that is unbreakable. Don't let setbacks discourage you. Use them as opportunities to learn and grow. Believe in yourself, and you will achieve great results.

You have a warrior's spirit within you. Use it to fight for your dreams, to overcome your fears, and to create the life you envision. You are strong, and you are capable of greatness. Your uniqueness is your superpower. Embrace what sets you apart, have confidence in your individuality, and let your true self shine. You are beautiful, inside and out. Confidence is not about knowing you will succeed; it's about knowing that even when you fail, you have the strength to bounce back. Have faith in yourself, and you will conquer any challenge. You are a living testament to the power of perseverance. Keep pushing your limits, keep believing in yourself, and let your resilience pave the way for your success.

You are deserving of love, especially from yourself. Embrace your flaws, acknowledge your strengths, and remember that self-love is the foundation for a happy and fulfilling life. Never forget that you are enough just as you are. Embrace your uniqueness, celebrate your achievements, and shower yourself with love and compassion. You are worthy of all the love in the world.

Your worth is not defined by your accomplishments, your appearance, or the opinions of others. Love yourself unconditionally, and watch as your self-confidence soars. Self-love is not selfish; it is necessary for your well-being. Embrace your flaws, value your worth, and treat yourself with kindness and respect. You are deserving of love, especially from yourself.

You are a force to be reckoned with. Embrace your power, embrace your potential, and let your determination empower you to achieve the extraordinary.

You have the power to create the life you desire. Embrace your strengths, embrace your passions, and let your actions empower you to make a difference in the world.

Your happiness is a reflection of your mindset. Choose positivity, choose self-love, and let your positive energy attract all that you desire in life. Never underestimate the influence you have. Your words, your actions, and your presence can empower others to rise. Use your voice, be bold, and inspire those around you.

– Luciano Layne

Foreword

If the Art of War and the 48 Laws of Power
were brought together, this book is the result of the brilliant
principles that have shaped cultures and leaders for generations.

In this book are 50 laws that will provide insight into the hearts
and minds of every successful leader. If you are searching for ways
to be more influential and more powerful in your circles, these
laws are the foundation for success.

**In order to understand this book you must be willing to be
strategic in how you read and think and calculated in how you
apply each principle.**

This book is designed to be easy to digest and establishes
additional principles for immediate application into your daily life.
Each chapter is a different law and a breakdown of how that law
can be applied in different situations, how that law was formed,
and the reason it matters.

We are often faced with choices in our lives that force us to
choose taking a difficult path riddled with challenges for our
personal growth and development or taking an easier way out that
allows us to remain comfortable in our current environment.

Only the most successful leaders intentionally choose to challenge
themselves. Personal growth and development is a lifelong
process that never ends. But, it must begin somewhere.

This book is intended to challenge you and give you a pathway to
becoming the best leader in any environment.

Contents

Contents

Introduction

In a world governed by influence and power, understanding the unwritten rules that dictate success is paramount. Drawing from history, psychology, and timeless wisdom, "The Code of Influence" presents fifty laws to navigate the complex landscape of power dynamics. From Machiavellian principles to modern strategies, this book is a guide for those seeking to wield power wisely and ethically.

Chapter 1: Law of Perception

"Control how you are perceived, for perception often shapes reality."

The idea that perception shapes reality is a powerful one. It underscores the importance of managing how others perceive you, as their perception can influence how they interact with you and ultimately shape your reality. It's a reminder to be mindful of the image you project and the impressions you leave on others.

Some of the theories that support the law of perception include:

1. Gestalt Principles: These principles describe how we perceive patterns and forms, such as similarity, proximity, closure, and continuity.

2. Depth Perception: This involves how we perceive the three-dimensional world, including cues like binocular disparity, relative size, and motion parallax.

3. Top-Down Processing: This refers to how our prior knowledge, expectations, and context influence our perception of stimuli.

4. Bottom-Up Processing: This is the opposite, where perception begins with the stimulus itself, and our brain processes the sensory information without influence from prior knowledge or expectations.

Understanding the principles found in the "Law of Perception", helps shed light on how our minds interpret the world around us.

Chapter 2: Law of Authority

"Establish yourself as an authority figure to command respect and influence."

Establishing yourself as an authority figure can indeed be a powerful tool for commanding respect and influencing others. Whether in professional settings, personal relationships, or societal contexts, people tend to defer to those they perceive as knowledgeable and authoritative. It involves building expertise, confidence, and credibility to effectively lead and guide others.

Below is a breakdown of the law of authority from a psychological standpoint:

1. Compliance with Authority: People are more likely to comply with requests or commands given by someone they perceive as an authority figure. This compliance can occur even if the request goes against their personal beliefs or values.

2. Milgram's Obedience Experiments: Stanley Milgram conducted experiments in the 1960s to study obedience to authority. Participants were instructed to administer electric shocks to others (actors pretending to be participants) under the guise of a scientific study. Despite hearing screams of pain from the actors, many participants continued to administer shocks when instructed to do so by the experimenter (an authority figure).

3. Factors Influencing Compliance: Several factors influence the degree of compliance with authority, including the perceived legitimacy of the authority figure, the presence of other obedient

individuals, and the immediacy of the situation.

4. Implications: The law of authority has significant implications for understanding human behavior, particularly in situations where authority figures wield power over others, such as in hierarchical organizations, legal settings, and social contexts.

Overall the "Law of Authority" sheds light on the powerful influence authority figures can have on individual behavior and decision-making processes.

Chapter 3: Law of Strategy

"Plan meticulously and adapt swiftly to outmaneuver your opponents."

The law of strategy emphasizes the importance of both careful planning and the ability to adapt quickly. By meticulously planning your actions and anticipating potential challenges, you can position yourself to outmaneuver opponents. However, being able to adapt swiftly in the face of changing circumstances is crucial for maintaining an advantage and achieving success.

When referring to the law of strategy we're referring to principles that govern effective strategic planning and decision making. Listed below is a breakdown of how this strategy looks in a practical sense:

1. Goal Alignment: A strategic plan starts with clearly defined goals and objectives that align with the overall mission or purpose of an organization or individual.

2. Analysis: This involves assessing internal and external factors that could impact the achievement of goals. This includes analyzing strengths, weaknesses, opportunities, and threats (SWOT analysis), as well as market trends, competitor behavior, and other relevant factors.

3. Resource Allocation: Effective strategy involves allocating resources such as time, money, and manpower in a way that maximizes their impact on achieving the stated goals.

4. Risk Management: Anticipating and mitigating potential risks and uncertainties is crucial in strategic planning. This involves identifying potential obstacles and developing contingency plans to address them.

5. Monitoring and Evaluation: Regular monitoring and evaluation of progress are essential to ensure that the strategy remains on track and to identify areas for improvement or adjustment.

By following the principals laid out in the "Law of Strategy", individuals and organizations can develop and implement strategies that increase their likelihood of success in achieving their goals.

Chapter 4: Law of Discretion

"Reveal information selectively, for knowledge is power."

The law of discretion highlights the strategic use of information. By revealing information selectively, you can maintain control over the narrative and leverage knowledge to your advantage. In many situations, withholding certain information can give you an edge and preserve your power in negotiations, decision-making, and interactions with others.

A deeper look at the nuances of the law of discretion:

1. Authority and Responsibility: Discretion often involves individuals being entrusted with the authority to make decisions within a certain scope of responsibility. This authority comes with the expectation that decisions will be made judiciously and in the best interest of the organization, group, or individuals involved.

2. Decision-Making: Discretion encompasses the process of decision-making, which involves assessing available options, considering relevant factors and potential consequences, and ultimately choosing a course of action. This process may require weighing conflicting interests, balancing competing priorities, and navigating uncertainty.

3. Ethical Considerations: In exercising discretion, individuals are often called upon to consider ethical principles and values. this may involve evaluating the potential impact of decisions on stakeholders, adhering to professional codes of conduct, and

upholding moral standards.

4. Context Sensitivity: Discretion is often context-dependent, meaning that the appropriateness of a decision may vary depending on the specific circumstances. Factors such as cultural norms, legal requirements, organizational policies, and situational dynamics can influence the exercise of discretion.

5. Accountability: Although discretion grants individuals the freedom to make decisions, it also entails accountability for those decisions. Individuals may be held accountable for the outcomes of their discretionary actions, particularly if they fail to exercise due diligence, act negligently, or violate established norms or regulations.

Overall, the "Law of Discretion" underscores the importance of thoughtful decision making and responsible judgement, particularly in situations where individuals have the autonomy to exercise discretion.

Chapter 5: Law of Alliances

"Form strategic alliances to amplify your influence and protect your interests."

The law of alliances underscores the importance of forming strategic partnerships to strengthen your influence and safeguard your interests. By aligning with others who share your goals or have complementary strengths, you can pool resources, expertise, and support to achieve mutual objectives. Building alliances can also provide a layer of protection and enhance your ability to navigate complex challenges effectively.

A breakdown of the different applications:

1. Business: In business, forming alliances with other companies can be strategic for mutual benefit, such as in joint ventures, partnerships, or strategic alliances. This could involve sharing resources, expertise, or markets to achieve common goals.

2. International Relations: In geopolitics, alliances between nations can shape global dynamics, influence diplomatic relations, and impact security strategies. Alliances may be formalized through treaties or informal agreements based on shared interests or geopolitical considerations.

3. Social Dynamics: In social settings, alliances can form among individuals or groups based on common interests, goals, or identities. These alliances may be temporary or long-lasting and can influence social networks, group dynamics, and collective actions.

4. Game Theory: In game theory, alliances can emerge in competitive environments where players seek to maximize their outcomes. Forming alliances with others may provide strategic advantages, such as increased bargaining power or protection against threats.

Overall, the "Law of Alliances" involves cooperation, collaboration, and strategic partnerships among entities with shared interests or objectives. These alliances can vary in nature and purpose depending on the context in which they occur.

Chapter 6: Law of Timing

"Seize the opportune moment to maximize the impact of your actions."

The law of timing emphasizes the critical importance of seizing the right moment to take action. By being attuned to timing, you can maximize the impact of your efforts and capitalize on favorable circumstances. Whether in business, relationships, or personal endeavors, knowing when to act can make all the difference in achieving success and realizing your goals.

While the law of timing is not a specific psychological or scientific principal, it is vital in various contexts. Below is a deeper look at the influence of timing in various applications:

1. Strategic Planning: Timing is crucial in strategic planning and execution. This involves identifying the optimal time to take action, such as launching a new product, entering a market, or making a strategic move in a competitive environment. Timing can significantly impact the success or failure of a strategy.

2. Decision-Making: Timing plays a role in decision-making processes. Knowing when to make a decision, whether to act quickly or wait for more information, can influence outcomes. Effective Decision makers consider the urgency of the situation, the availability of resources , and potential consequences when determining the timing of their decisions.

3. Interpersonal Relationships: This includes knowing when to communicate important information, offer support, or address

conflicts. Being sensitive to the emotional state and circumstances of others can help in choosing the right timing for interactions.

4. Opportunity Recognition: Recognizing opportunities requires a keen sense of timing. Whether in business, career, or personal life, seizing opportunities often depends on being in the right place at the right time and taking action when the timing is favorable.

5. Adaptability: Timing involves not only knowing when to act but also being adaptable and responsive to changes in timing. Circumstances can shift, and what may have been the right timing initially may no longer be optimal. Flexibility and the ability to adjust plans accordingly are essential.

Overall, the "Law of Timing" underscores the importance of considering timing factors in all facets of life in order to maximize effectiveness and success.

Chapter 7: Law of Ambition

"Cultivate unrelenting ambition to fuel your journey to power."

The law of ambition highlights the relentless drive and determination needed to pursue power and success. Cultivating unrelenting ambition provides the motivation and energy to overcome obstacles, push boundaries, and achieve your goals. It's about setting high aspirations, staying focused, and continually striving for growth and advancement in all aspects of life.

Ambition can often be associated with a variety of feelings. Depending on the context it can be seen as good or bad. Below are a few ways to interpret ambition:

1. Personal Drive: Ambition is often seen as a personal drive or desire to achieve success, reach goals, or fulfill one's potential. This drive can push individuals to work hard, take risks, and overcome obstacles in pursuit of their aspirations.

2. Motivational Force: Ambition serves as a powerful motivational force, propelling individuals to strive for excellence and pursue opportunities for growth and advancement. It can inspire innovation, creativity, and perseverance in the face of challenges.

3. Goal Setting: Ambitious individuals often set challenging goals for themselves, pushing the boundaries of what they believe is possible. These goals serve as benchmarks for progress and provide direction for their efforts.

4. Risk-Taking: Ambition often involves a willingness to take calculated risks in pursuit of one's goals. This may involve stepping outside comfort zones, embracing uncertainty, and being open to failure as a learning opportunity.

5. Ethical Considerations: Ambition should be tempered by a sense of morality and responsibility to ensure that success is achieved ethically and without harm to others.

6. Balance and Well-Being: It's important for individuals to balance ambition with other aspects of life, such as relationships, health, and well-being. Overly ambitious pursuits can lead to burnout, stress, or neglect of other important areas of life.

Overall, the "Law of Ambition" reflects the powerful force that ambition can be in driving individuals to pursue their goals and aspirations, while also highlighting the importance of balance, ethics, and well-being amidst the pursuit of their goals.

Chapter 8: Law of Adaptation

"Adapt to changing circumstances and thrive in adversity."

The law of adaptation underscores the importance of being flexible and resilient in the face of changing circumstances. By adapting to adversity, you can not only survive but also thrive in challenging situations. This involves being open to new strategies, adjusting your approach as needed, and finding opportunities for growth and innovation even in the most difficult times.

Adaptation is a word used in various contexts. When applied in various contexts it can provide a complete narrative of how we ought to navigate the process of adapting to change. Below are a wide range of examples of adaptation:

1. Biological Evolution: In biology, adaptation refers to the process by which organisms change over time to better suit their environment. This can involve physiological, behavioral, or anatomical changes that increase an organism's chances of survival and reproduction in a given environment.

2. Psychological Adaptation: In psychology, adaptation can refer to the process by which individuals adjust to new or changing circumstances. This can involve cognitive, emotional, or behavioral changes that help individuals cope with challenges, navigate social situations, and achieve well-being.

3. Societal and Cultural Adaptation: Societies and cultures also undergo adaptation in response to changes in their environment,

technology, demographics, and other factors. This can involve shifts in social norms, values, institutions, and practices to better meet the needs of the population and address emerging challenges.

4. Organizational Adaptation: In business and organizational contexts, adaptation involves adjusting strategies, structures, processes, and practices in response to changes in the external environment or internal conditions. This may include innovations, restructuring, and other forms of organizational change to remain competitive and sustainable.

5. Personal Adaptation: On an individual level, adaptation involves the ability to adjust to life's challenges, transitions, and uncertainties. This can include developing resilience, flexibility, problem-solving skills, and coping mechanisms to effectively navigate life's ups and downs.

Overall, the "Law of Adaptation" highlights the importance of flexibility, resilience, and change in various domains of life, from biological evolution to individual behavior to societal dynamics. Adaptation is a fundamental process that enables organisms, societies, and organizations to thrive in a dynamic and ever-changing world.

Chapter 9: Law of Humility

"Humility leads to strength and not to weakness. It is the highest form of respect"

The Law of Humility emphasizes the importance of modesty, self-awareness, and openness to learning. It suggests that individuals should acknowledge their limitations, accept constructive criticism, and be willing to learn from others. Practicing humility involves recognizing that one's knowledge and perspective are limited and that there is always more to understand and explore.

We all know someone who believes they are humble, but what does humility really look like? Below is a breakdown humility as an attribute of one's character:

1. Acceptance of Imperfection: Humility involves accepting one's imperfections and recognizing that everyone makes mistakes.

2. Empathy and Compassion: Humility fosters a sense of compassion and understanding, leading to more meaningful and respectful interactions.

3. Gratitude: Humility often goes hand in hand with gratitude, as it involves acknowledging the contributions of others and being grateful for the opportunities and experiences one has been given.

4. Openness to Feedback: Feedback is an opportunity for growth and improvement rather than a threat to the ego.

5. Servant Leadership: Leaders should prioritize the needs of

others and empower their team members. Humble leaders lead by example, fostering a culture of collaboration and mutual respect.

6. Lifelong Learning: Humility encourages a mindset of lifelong learning and curiosity. It involves being open to new ideas, perspectives, and experiences.

7. Balance of Confidence and Humility: Humility does not mean lacking confidence or self-esteem. Rather, it involves striking a balance between confidence in one's abilities and a recognition of one's limitations, leading to a more grounded and authentic sense of self.

Overall, the "Law of Humility" promotes a mindset of humility and openness that fosters personal growth, meaningful relationships, and positive contributions to society. It enables the practitioner to be a lifelong learner and expand their network to enable them to pursue success with the strength of their cohort.

Chapter 10: Law of Influence

"Influence others subtly, for overt manipulation breeds resistance."

The law of influence suggests that subtle influence is often more effective than overt manipulation. By subtly guiding others through persuasion, empathy, and authenticity, you can gain their trust and cooperation without triggering resistance. Building genuine connections and inspiring others to willingly align with your goals can lead to more sustainable and positive outcomes in relationships and interactions.

The law of influence can be understood in various ways:

1. Social Influence: In psychology, the concept of influence refers to the ability of one person or group to affect the attitudes, beliefs, or behaviors of others. This can occur through direct persuasion, social norms, or the presence of authority figures.

2. Principles of Influence: Psychologist Robert Cialdini identified several principles of influence, including reciprocity (the tendency to feel obligated to repay others for favors), commitment and consistency (the desire to align behavior with previous commitments), social proof (the tendency to follow the actions of others), authority (the tendency to comply with figures of authority), liking (the tendency to comply with requests from people we like), and scarcity (the tendency to value scarce resources more highly).

3. Leadership Influence: Effective leaders understand how to leverage their influence to inspire, motivate, and guide others

toward common goals through their actions, decisions, and communication styles.

4. Cultural Influence: Cultural influencers such as celebrities, artists, and thought leaders can have a profound impact on society by shaping attitudes, trends, and beliefs.

5. Ethical Considerations: While influence can be a powerful tool for effecting change, it's important to consider the ethical implications of using influence to persuade or manipulate others. Ethical influence involves transparency, honesty, and respect for the autonomy and well-being of others.

Overall, the "Law of Influence" underscores the pervasive nature of social influence and its impact on individual and collective behavior. Understanding the principles of influence can help individuals navigate social interactions, leadership roles, and decision-making processes more effectively.

Chapter 11: Law of Control

"Maintain control over your emotions, actions, and environment."

The law of control emphasizes the importance of maintaining control over your emotions, actions, and environment. By mastering self-discipline, staying composed in challenging situations, and exerting influence over your surroundings, you can navigate life with greater efficiency and resilience. This involves managing impulses, making deliberate choices, and taking proactive steps to shape your circumstances rather than being controlled by them.

The law of control is more of an art than a scientific principle. Below is a breakdown of our understanding of control from various viewpoints:

1. Personal Agency: The law of control could refer to the concept of personal agency, which involves individuals' beliefs about their ability to control their own actions, behaviors, and outcomes. Having a sense of control over one's life can lead to greater well-being, motivation, and resilience.

2. Locus of Control: In psychology, locus of control refers to individuals' beliefs about the extent to which they can control events in their lives. People with an internal locus of control believe they have control over their destinies, while those with an external locus of control believe that outcomes are determined by external factors such as luck, fate, or powerful others.

3. Control Theory: Control theory is a psychological theory that suggests that individuals are motivated to maintain a sense of control over their environments. This theory posits that when individuals perceive a discrepancy between their current state and a desired state, they are motivated to take action to regain control and reduce the discrepancy.

4. Social Control: In sociology, social control refers to the mechanisms, institutions, and processes through which societies regulate individual and group behavior to maintain order and stability. Social control can be exerted through formal mechanisms such as laws and regulations, as well as informal mechanisms such as social norms, values, and peer pressure.

Overall, the "Law of Control" can encompass various aspects related to personal agency, beliefs about control, and social mechanisms of control. It underscores the importance of understanding how individuals perceive and exert control over their lives and the environments in which they live.

Chapter 12: Law of Persuasion

"Master the art of persuasion through rhetoric, psychology, and negotiation."

The law of persuasion highlights the mastery of various techniques such as rhetoric, psychology, and negotiation to influence others effectively. By understanding the principles behind persuasion and employing them strategically, you can sway opinions, inspire action, and achieve your objectives. This involves crafting compelling arguments, appealing to emotions, and finding common ground to build consensus and create win-win outcomes.

The "Law of Persuasion" encompasses various psychological and communication strategies used to influence others' beliefs, attitudes, and behaviors. Here's a breakdown:

1.   Principles of Persuasion: Psychologist Robert Cialdini outlined several principles of persuasion, including reciprocity (the tendency to feel obligated to repay favors), commitment and consistency (the desire to align behavior with previous commitments), social proof (the tendency to follow the actions of others), authority (the tendency to comply with figures of authority), liking (the tendency to comply with requests from people we like), and scarcity (the tendency to value scarce resources more highly).

2.   Communication Techniques: Effective persuasion often involves employing various communication techniques, such as framing (presenting information in a way that emphasizes certain aspects), storytelling (using narratives to convey messages and

evoke emotions), and rhetorical devices (such as repetition, rhetorical questions, and appeals to emotion).

3. Understanding Audiences: Persuasion is more effective when tailored to the audience's attitudes, beliefs, values, and motivations. This requires understanding the audience's needs and concerns and framing messages in a way that resonates with them.

4. Ethical Considerations: While persuasion can be used for positive purposes, such as promoting health behaviors or advocating for social change, it's important to consider the ethical implications of persuasion techniques. Ethical persuasion involves transparency, honesty, and respect for the autonomy and well-being of others.

Overall, the "Law of Persuasion" highlights the complex interplay of psychological, communication, and ethical factors involved in influencing others' beliefs and behaviors. Understanding the principles and techniques of persuasion can help individuals and organizations effectively communicate their messages and achieve their goals.

Chapter 13: Law of Deconstruction

"Analyze your beliefs to understand how they affect your reality"

The Law of Deconstruction suggests that there is value in analyzing one's beliefs in order to find the source of those beliefs and reevaluate if they continue to be true. Deconstruction involves analyzing beliefs to uncover hidden assumptions, contradictions, and ambiguities, so that the observer can reorganize or affirm their beliefs in light of new knowledge. While new beliefs may be formed, deconstruction is intended to be an educational process for old beliefs and new beliefs alike.

Here is a breakdown of how deconstruction can be valuable in a variety of situations:

1. Deconstruction in the Workplace: Companies and organizations often have mantras and statements that are the backbone of the business. It is wise to review these mantras every few years to evaluate if they are still true or if they need to be adapted.

2. Deconstruction in the Home: Households often fall into patterns of thinking that are passed down from generation to generation. These lines of thought can be beneficial or harmful if they are not revisited and processed through in light of the ever changing environment of individuals.

3. Deconstruction in Politics: The process of analyzing commonly

held principals, uncovering the truth behind political motivations, and applying current information can be applied to expose power dynamics, hierarchies, and ideologies embedded within government systems and business structures.

 6. Continual Process: Deconstruction is not a method with a fixed set of rules, but rather a continual process of questioning and destabilizing meaning. It is a mode of critical inquiry that encourages openness to multiple interpretations and perspectives.

Overall, the "Law of Deconstruction" is intended to expose the complex interactions of psychological, communication, and ethical factors involved in the environments we find ourselves in. Understanding the motivation behind our beliefs and contrasting them in light of new found information is always a wise practice. However, the practitioner must be careful not to abandon their beliefs at the first sign of discrepancies, but push through those initial feelings of shock to reach the base in which to build their belief system once again.

Chapter 14: Law of Leverage

"Utilize resources, relationships, and leverage points to amplify your influence."

The law of leverage emphasizes the strategic utilization of resources, relationships, and leverage points to amplify your influence. By identifying and harnessing these assets effectively, you can magnify the impact of your efforts and achieve greater results. Whether it's capitalizing on existing networks, leveraging expertise, or exploiting advantageous positions, mastering the art of leverage can significantly enhance your ability to succeed and exert influence in various domains.

Below is a breakdown of the various uses of the word leverage across multiple disciplines to provide a complete context for how leverage can be applied in your situation:

1. Mechanical Advantage: In physics and engineering, leverage refers to the mechanical advantage gained by using a lever or other tool to amplify force. The law of leverage states that a small force applied at the right point can move a much larger object.

2. Business and Finance: In business and finance, leverage refers to the use of borrowed capital to increase the potential return on investment. The law of leverage suggests that using debt or leverage can amplify profits, but it also increases the risk of losses.

3. Productivity and Efficiency: In personal and professional development, leverage can refer to strategies for maximizing productivity and efficiency. This could involve identifying key

leverage points where a small change can lead to significant improvements in outcomes.

 4. Influence and Impact: Leverage can also refer to the ability to exert influence or achieve greater impact with minimal effort. This could involve leveraging relationships, resources, or expertise to achieve desired outcomes.

Overall, the "Law of Leverage" underscores the importance of strategic thinking, resource allocation, and efficiency in various domains, from physics and engineering to business and personal development. It emphasizes the potential for achieving greater results with less effort by identifying and leveraging key opportunities and resources.

Chapter 15: Law of Ethics

"Navigate power dynamics with integrity and ethical conduct."

The law of ethics underscores the importance of navigating power dynamics with integrity and ethical conduct. Regardless of the pursuit of power or influence, maintaining a commitment to moral principles and treating others with fairness, honesty, and respect is essential. Upholding ethical standards not only fosters trust and credibility but also ensures sustainable success and positive outcomes in both personal and professional endeavors.

The "Law of Ethics" generally refers to the principles and standards of conduct that govern individual and organizational behavior. Here's a breakdown:

1. Ethical Principles: Ethics involves principles that guide behavior, such as honesty, integrity, fairness, and respect for others. These principles serve as a moral compass for individuals and organizations, helping them make decisions that align with values and contribute to the greater good.

2. Codes of Ethics: Many professions and organizations have codes of ethics that outline expected standards of behavior and conduct for members or employees. These codes often provide guidance on issues such as confidentiality, conflicts of interest, and professional integrity.

3. Ethical Decision-Making: Ethical decision-making involves considering the potential impact of actions on stakeholders,

evaluating alternatives, and choosing courses of action that are consistent with ethical principles and values. This process may involve weighing competing interests and navigating ethical dilemmas.

4. Social Responsibility: Ethical behavior extends beyond individual actions to encompass broader social responsibility. Organizations are increasingly expected to consider the ethical implications of their decisions and actions on society, the environment, and future generations.

5. Enforcement and Accountability: Upholding ethical standards requires mechanisms for enforcement and accountability. This may involve disciplinary measures for unethical behavior, transparency in decision-making processes, and mechanisms for reporting unethical conduct.

Overall, the "Law of Ethics" emphasizes the importance of ethical behavior in promoting trust, integrity, and respect in individual and organizational interactions. It underscores the need for individuals and organizations to uphold ethical principles and values in their actions and decisions in order to achieve their highest potential.

Chapter 16: Law of Mastery

"Strive for mastery in your chosen domain to establish dominance and authority."

The law of mastery emphasizes the pursuit of excellence and expertise in your chosen domain as a means to establish dominance and authority. By dedicating yourself to continuous learning, practice, and refinement, you can elevate your skills to a level that sets you apart from others. Mastery not only commands respect and admiration but also affords you the confidence and competence to lead and influence others effectively within your field of expertise.

"Law of Mastery" can be broken down in various ways:

1.   Continuous Improvement: Mastery often involves the pursuit of continuous improvement and excellence in a particular skill, discipline, or domain. This may require dedication, practice, and a willingness to learn and grow over time.

2.   Deliberate Practice: Achieving mastery often involves deliberate practice, which entails focused, goal-oriented practice aimed at improving specific aspects of performance. Deliberate practice involves seeking feedback, identifying areas for improvement, and pushing oneself beyond one's comfort zone.

3.   Expertise and Specialization: Mastery may involve becoming an expert or specialist in a particular field or domain. This may require deep knowledge, skills, and experience within that domain, as well as the ability to innovate and push the

boundaries of what is known or possible.

4. Lifelong Learning: Mastery is often seen as a journey rather than a destination, requiring ongoing learning, adaptation, and growth. Those who strive for mastery are committed to lifelong learning and development, continuously seeking to refine their skills and knowledge.

5. Legacy and Impact: Mastery can also involve leaving a lasting legacy and making a significant impact in one's field or community. Those who achieve mastery may inspire and influence others, passing on their knowledge and expertise to future generations.

Overall, the "Law of Mastery" emphasizes the importance of dedication, practice, and lifelong learning in achieving excellence and making a meaningful impact in one's chosen field or domain. It underscores the idea that mastery is not an end goal, but a journey of continuous improvement and growth.

Chapter 17: Law of Subtlety

"Operate with subtlety and finesse to avoid unnecessary conflict and scrutiny."

The law of subtlety suggests that operating with subtlety and finesse can help you avoid unnecessary conflict and scrutiny. By navigating situations with tact, diplomacy, and discretion, you can minimize resistance and maintain a low profile when needed. This approach allows you to achieve your goals with less friction, while also preserving relationships and reputation.

The "Law of Subtlety" is a nuanced principle. It crosses multiple fields of discipline as demonstrated below:

1.   Communication: In communication, subtlety refers to the use of indirect or nuanced language, gestures, or cues to convey meaning. This could involve subtly influencing others' perceptions, attitudes, or behaviors through subtle cues or messages.

2.   Psychology: In psychology, subtlety can refer to subtle cues or signals that influence perception, decision-making, and behavior. This could include subconscious influences, priming effects, or subtle manipulation tactics.

3.   Art and Aesthetics: In art and aesthetics, subtlety can refer to the use of understated or nuanced elements to convey meaning, evoke emotion, or create impact. This could involve subtle changes in color, composition, or texture that are not immediately obvious but contribute to the overall effect.

4. Strategy and Tactics: In strategy and tactics, subtlety can refer to the use of strategic maneuvers or subtle tactics to achieve objectives. This could involve subtle shifts in approach, timing, or positioning that are not immediately apparent but have significant impact on outcomes.

Overall, the "Law of Subtlety" suggests that subtle influences, cues, or strategies can have significant effects on perception, behavior, and outcomes. It underscores the importance of paying attention to subtle nuances and cues in various contexts to better understand and navigate complex situations.

Chapter 18: Law of Seduction

"Win over hearts and minds through charm, allure, and persuasion."

The law of seduction emphasizes the art of winning over hearts and minds through charm, allure, and persuasion. By mastering the techniques of attraction and influence, you can captivate others and inspire their loyalty and admiration. Whether in personal relationships, business negotiations, or social interactions, the ability to charm and persuade can be a powerful tool for achieving your objectives and building meaningful connections.

The "Law of Seduction" uses the physical to influence and steer the cognitive. Below is a breakdown of how seduction can play a role in various dynamics:

1. Social Dynamics: In interpersonal relationships, seduction refers to the process of enticing, attracting, or captivating someone emotionally, physically, or intellectually. This can involve using charm, charisma, and persuasive tactics to create a sense of desire or attraction.

2. Psychological Influence: Seduction can also involve psychological tactics aimed at influencing someone's thoughts, emotions, or behavior. This could include techniques such as flattery, mirroring, and creating a sense of mystery or allure.

3. Ethical Considerations: While seduction can be used positively to foster genuine connections and intimacy, it's important to consider the ethical implications of using seductive tactics. Ethical

seduction involves transparency, honesty, and respect for the autonomy and well-being of others.

4. Personal Development: Some individuals may study seduction techniques as part of personal development or self-improvement efforts. This could involve learning social skills, confidence-building techniques, and strategies for attracting and connecting with others.

5. Cultural and Artistic Expression: Seduction is a common theme in literature, art, and popular culture, often depicted as a form of romantic or sexual allure. It can be explored as a complex and multifaceted aspect of human interaction and expression.

Overall, the "Law of Seduction" highlights the intricate dynamics of attraction, persuasion, and influence in human relationships. It underscores the importance of understanding and navigating these dynamics with integrity, empathy, and respect for others.

Chapter 19: Law of Disruption

"Disrupt the status quo to create opportunities for growth and advancement."

The law of disruption encourages challenging the status quo to create opportunities for growth and advancement. By breaking away from conventional thinking and methods, you can identify new paths, innovate, and drive change in your environment. Embracing disruption allows you to stay ahead of the curve, seize emerging opportunities, and carve out a unique position in your industry or field.

The "Law of Disruption" is often used to describe the phenomenon of disruptive innovation or change in various contexts:

1. Business and Technology: In business and technology, the law of disruption refers to the process by which innovative products, services, or business models disrupt existing markets or industries. This disruption often occurs when new entrants introduce simpler, more affordable, or more convenient alternatives to existing solutions, challenging established incumbents.

2. Creative Destruction: The law of disruption is sometimes associated with the concept of creative destruction, coined by economist Joseph Schumpeter. Creative destruction refers to the process by which new innovations and technologies replace or render obsolete existing products, industries, or ways of doing business.

3. Social and Cultural Change: Disruption can also occur in social and cultural contexts, leading to shifts in norms, values, and behaviors. This could involve movements for social justice, cultural revolutions, or changes in consumer preferences that disrupt traditional institutions, practices, or beliefs.

4. Personal Growth and Transformation: On an individual level, disruption can be a catalyst for personal growth and transformation. It may involve stepping out of comfort zones, challenging limiting beliefs, and embracing change as an opportunity for learning and development.

5. Resilience and Adaptation: Dealing with disruption often requires resilience, adaptability, and a willingness to embrace uncertainty. Individuals and organizations that can effectively navigate disruption are better positioned to thrive in dynamic and unpredictable environments.

Overall, the "Law of Disruption" underscores the inevitability of change and the importance of embracing innovation, adaptation, and resilience in responding to disruptive forces. It highlights the potential for disruption to drive progress, growth, and transformation in various domains of life.

Chapter 20: Law of Unity

"Unify diverse interests and factions to consolidate power and influence."

The law of unity emphasizes the importance of unifying diverse interests and factions to consolidate power and influence. By bringing together disparate groups and aligning their goals, you can create a stronger, more cohesive entity that wields greater collective strength. This involves fostering cooperation, building bridges, and finding common ground to forge alliances that advance shared objectives while also enhancing your own position of power and influence.

The "Law of Unity" is a gathering principle. Below are some practical examples of how different applications lead to universal success amongst the participants:

1. Social Cohesion: In sociology and psychology, the law of unity refers to the idea that individuals or groups are stronger and more effective when they are united in purpose, values, or goals. Unity fosters social cohesion, cooperation, and collective action, leading to shared success and well-being.

2. Teamwork and Collaboration: In organizations and teams, the law of unity emphasizes the importance of collaboration, communication, and alignment toward common objectives. When individuals work together toward a shared goal, they can leverage their diverse skills, perspectives, and resources to achieve greater results.

3. Community and Solidarity: The law of unity can also apply to communities and societies, highlighting the importance of solidarity, mutual support, and inclusivity. When members of a community come together in unity, they can address collective challenges, promote social justice, and foster a sense of belonging and connectedness.

4. Spiritual and Philosophical Perspectives: In spiritual and philosophical traditions, the law of unity may refer to the interconnectedness of all beings and the underlying unity of existence. This perspective emphasizes the interdependence and oneness of all life forms, transcending differences and divisions.

Overall, the "Law of Unity" underscores the power of cooperation, collaboration, and solidarity in promoting harmony, progress, and well-being in various spheres of life. It highlights the importance of recognizing and celebrating our shared humanity while embracing diversity and inclusivity.

Chapter 21: Law of Deception

"Employ strategic deception sparingly and judiciously to achieve your objectives."

The law of deception suggests using strategic deception sparingly and judiciously to achieve your objectives. While deception can be a powerful tactic in certain situations, overuse or misuse can lead to distrust and backlash. Therefore, employing deception strategically, with careful consideration of its potential consequences, can help you navigate complex scenarios and gain an advantage while minimizing negative repercussions.

The "Law of Deception" is a controversial principal according to many. However, when applied appropriately it is not rooted in malice, but in a delayed revelation that leads to success in due time. Below is a breakdown of deception and its uses:

1. Psychology: In psychology, deception refers to the act of misleading or manipulating others through false or misleading information. This could involve lying, withholding information, or presenting a distorted version of reality to achieve personal gain or advantage.

2. Social Interactions: Deception can occur in various social interactions, such as negotiations, relationships, or competitive settings. Individuals may use deception to gain advantage, protect themselves, or avoid negative consequences.

3. Ethics and Morality: Deception raises ethical and moral questions about honesty, integrity, and trustworthiness. While

some forms of deception may be considered acceptable or even necessary in certain situations (e.g., white lies to spare someone's feelings), deliberate deception for personal gain or harm is generally considered unethical.

4. Detection and Countermeasures: Understanding the principles of deception can help individuals and organizations detect and counter deceptive tactics. This may involve critical thinking, skepticism, and awareness of common deception techniques.

5. Self-Deception: Deception can also occur internally, in the form of self-deception or cognitive biases that distort one's perceptions, beliefs, or judgments. Overcoming self-deception often requires self-awareness, introspection, and critical reflection.

Overall, the "Law of Deception" underscores the complexity of human interactions and the importance of honesty, transparency, and integrity in fostering trust and mutual respect. It also highlights the need for vigilance and critical thinking to navigate situations where deception may be present.

Chapter 22: Law of Innovation

"Innovate relentlessly to stay ahead of the competition and shape the future."

The law of innovation stresses the importance of relentless innovation to maintain a competitive edge and shape the future. By continuously seeking new ideas, technologies, and approaches, you can stay ahead of the curve, adapt to changing environments, and lead the way in your industry or field. Innovation not only drives progress and growth but also positions you as a visionary and thought leader, enabling you to influence and shape the direction of your industry or area of expertise.

The "Law of Innovation" encompasses various concepts related to the process of innovation and its impact:

1. Continuous Improvement: The law of innovation emphasizes the importance of continuous improvement and adaptation to changing circumstances. Innovation involves the creation and implementation of new ideas, processes, products, or services that improve upon existing ones.

2. Creative Problem-Solving: Innovation often involves creative problem-solving and thinking outside the box to develop novel solutions to challenges or opportunities. This may require experimentation, risk-taking, and openness to new ideas.

3. Disruption and Change: Innovation can lead to disruption and change in various industries, markets, and societies. Disruptive innovations challenge established norms, practices, and business

models, often leading to shifts in power, competition, and consumer behavior.

4. Entrepreneurship and Intrapreneurship: Innovation is often associated with entrepreneurship, as entrepreneurs identify opportunities and create value through innovative ideas and ventures. Intrapreneurship refers to innovation within existing organizations, where employees take initiative to develop and implement new ideas or projects.

5. Collaboration and Ecosystems: Innovation thrives in collaborative environments where diverse perspectives, expertise, and resources come together to drive progress. Innovation ecosystems encompass networks of organizations, individuals, institutions, and resources that support innovation and entrepreneurship.

6. Ethics and Impact: The law of innovation highlights the ethical considerations and societal impact of innovation. Innovations should be guided by principles of ethics, responsibility, and sustainability to ensure they benefit society and minimize negative consequences.

Overall, the "Law of Innovation" underscores the dynamic nature of innovation and its role in driving progress, economic growth, and societal development. It emphasizes the importance of creativity, collaboration, and ethical considerations in fostering a culture of innovation that addresses global challenges and improves quality of life.

Chapter 23: Law of Fear

"Inspire fear or respect, but never provoke unnecessary enmity."

The law of fear advises inspiring fear or respect when necessary but avoiding provoking unnecessary enmity. While instilling a sense of fear or respect can help establish authority and deter adversaries, unnecessarily antagonizing others can lead to backlash and undermine your objectives. Therefore, it's crucial to strike a balance, using fear or respect judiciously and strategically to maintain control and influence while minimizing unnecessary conflict.

The "Law of Fear" is a principle that should be exercised with caution and only when necessary. Understanding how to draw healthy fear is important for power dynamics:

1. Psychology: Fear is a natural emotion that alerts us to potential risks and triggers a fight-or-flight response, preparing us to either confront or avoid the threat.

2. Behavioral Economics: In behavioral economics, fear can influence decision-making processes and risk perceptions. The law of fear suggests that individuals may be more likely to avoid losses or negative outcomes than to pursue gains, a phenomenon known as loss aversion.

3. Social Control: Fear can be used as a tool for social control, where individuals or groups may use fear tactics to influence behavior, manipulate perceptions, or maintain power and control.

This could involve instilling fear through threats, propaganda, or coercion.

4. Self-Preservation: Fear serves an adaptive function by motivating individuals to take actions to protect themselves from harm or danger. This could involve seeking safety, avoiding risky situations, or seeking support from others in times of distress.

5. Overcoming Fear: While fear can be a natural response to threats, it can also be debilitating if it becomes excessive or irrational. Overcoming fear often involves facing fears gradually, challenging negative beliefs and perceptions, and developing coping strategies to manage anxiety and stress.

Overall, the "Law of Fear" highlights the complexities between psychological, social, and physiological factors in shaping our responses to perceived threats or dangers. Understanding fear can help individuals navigate challenges, make informed decisions, and cultivate resilience in the face of adversity.

Chapter 24: Law of Patience

"Cultivate patience and resilience in the face of setbacks and challenges."

The law of patience underscores the importance of cultivating patience and resilience when facing setbacks and challenges. By maintaining composure, staying focused on long-term goals, and persevering through difficulties, you can overcome obstacles and achieve success. Patience allows you to endure temporary setbacks and setbacks, while resilience empowers you to bounce back stronger and wiser, ultimately leading to greater growth and fulfillment in the journey toward your goals.

The "Law of Patience" embodies the concept of exercising patience in various aspects of life in order to press on to achievement of goals:

1. Personal Growth: The law of patience emphasizes the importance of patience in personal growth and development. It recognizes that progress often takes time and requires perseverance, resilience, and dedication.

2. Goal Achievement: Patience is essential for achieving long-term goals and aspirations. It involves staying committed to the journey, even when faced with setbacks or delays, and trusting that progress will come with consistent effort and persistence.

3. Relationships: Patience is crucial in nurturing healthy relationships, as it involves understanding, empathy, and tolerance for others' imperfections and differences. Patience allows space

for communication, forgiveness, and the gradual building of trust and intimacy.

4. Problem-Solving: Patience is valuable in problem-solving situations, as it encourages calmness, clarity of thought, and the ability to consider multiple perspectives and solutions. Rushing to find quick fixes may lead to hasty decisions or overlook important details.

5. Adversity and Challenges: Patience is particularly important during times of adversity and challenges. It involves maintaining a positive outlook, staying resilient, and trusting that difficult situations will eventually improve with time and effort.

6. Cultivating Inner Peace: Practicing patience can lead to greater inner peace and well-being. It involves accepting things as they are, letting go of the need for immediate gratification, and finding contentment in the present moment.

Overall, the "Law of Patience" underscores the value of patience in fostering personal growth, nurturing relationships, overcoming obstacles, and cultivating a sense of peace and fulfillment in life. It reminds us to embrace the journey, trust the process, and remain resilient in the face of life's challenges.

Chapter 25: Law of Secrecy

*"Guard your secrets closely, for knowledge
is a potent source of power."*

The law of secrecy advises guarding your secrets closely,
recognizing that knowledge is a potent source of power. By
keeping valuable information confidential, you maintain a
strategic advantage and control over the narrative. However, it's
important to discern when to share information selectively and
when to keep it hidden to maximize its impact and protect your
interests.

The "Law of Secrecy" can be combined with the law of deception.
Though they are similar in nature they vary in terms of application.
While secrecy is an action, deception is inaction. Below is.
breakdown:

1. Confidentiality: In some contexts, the law of secrecy refers to
the obligation to keep certain information confidential or secret.
This could include sensitive personal information, trade secrets,
classified government information, or proprietary business
information.

2. Security and Protection: Secrecy may be necessary to protect
individuals, organizations, or national security interests from harm
or exploitation. This could involve keeping plans, strategies, or
vulnerabilities secret to prevent them from falling into the wrong
hands.

3. Privacy: Secrecy can also relate to the right to privacy and the

ability to keep personal matters private from others. This could involve maintaining boundaries around personal information, activities, or relationships to preserve privacy and autonomy.

4. Manipulation and Deception: Secrecy can also be used for manipulative or deceptive purposes, where individuals or groups withhold information or conceal their intentions to gain an advantage or control over others.

5. Ethical Considerations: While secrecy may sometimes be necessary or justified, it raises ethical questions about transparency, accountability, and trust. There may be conflicts between the need for secrecy and the principles of openness, honesty, and integrity.

Overall, the "Law of Secrecy" highlights the complex ethical, legal, and practical considerations involved in keeping information confidential or secret. While secrecy may sometimes be necessary for security, privacy, or protection, it can also raise concerns about transparency, accountability, and trust in relationships and institutions. It is wise to only use secrecy when the benefits outweigh the potential damages.

Chapter 26: Law of Legacy

"Craft a legacy that endures beyond your lifetime, shaping history and memory."

The law of legacy encourages crafting a lasting impact that endures beyond your lifetime, shaping history and memory. By living with purpose, integrity, and vision, you can leave behind a meaningful legacy that influences future generations and contributes to positive change in the world. Whether through your achievements, contributions, or values, cultivating a legacy ensures that your impact continues to resonate long after you're gone, leaving a lasting imprint on the world.

The "Law of Legacy" is a principle that pushes the practitioner to think beyond their current existence. It forces the practitioner to understand that the weight of their actions goes beyond their current condition:

1. Impact and Influence: The law of legacy emphasizes the idea that individuals have the power to leave a lasting impact or imprint on the world. This could involve contributions to society, accomplishments in one's field, or the way one's actions and values influence others.

2. Generational Influence: Legacy can also refer to the influence passed down from one generation to the next. This includes family traditions, values, stories, and teachings that shape the identity and character of future generations.

3. Personal Branding: In personal branding and leadership, legacy

refers to the reputation, impact, and lasting impression an individual leaves on their industry, organization, or community. This involves cultivating a positive legacy through consistent actions, values, and contributions.

4. Social Change and Progress: Legacy can encompass efforts to create positive social change and progress in areas such as human rights, environmental sustainability, or global peace. This involves working towards a better future for future generations and leaving the world a better place than one found it.

5. Reflection and Intention: The law of legacy encourages individuals to reflect on their values, goals, and aspirations and consider how they want to be remembered. This involves living with intention, purpose, and integrity to create a meaningful legacy that aligns with one's values and vision for the future.

Overall, the "Law of Legacy" underscores the importance of considering the long-term impact of one's actions, decisions, and contributions. It encourages individuals to live with purpose, integrity, and a commitment to leaving the world a better place for future generations.

Chapter 27: Law of Accountability

"Accountability is the glue that ties commitment to results"

The law of accountability is essential to the success of any individual, business, or organization. Failure to accept responsibility for actions is the leading reason for stagnancy or deterioration. Accountability ensures that anyone involved is motivated towards the same goal with a proper measure of conviction for success.

The "Law of Accountability" emphasizes the importance of taking responsibility for one's actions, decisions, and their consequences. Here's a breakdown:

1. Personal Responsibility: Accountability starts with individuals acknowledging their roles and obligations in achieving personal and collective goals. It involves owning up to one's actions, admitting mistakes, and taking proactive steps to rectify any harm caused.

2. Ethical Standards: Accountability is closely linked to ethical conduct. Individuals and organizations are accountable for upholding ethical standards, integrity, and transparency in their interactions and operations. This includes being honest, fair, and respectful in all dealings.

3. Leadership: In leadership, accountability is essential for

fostering trust, credibility, and effectiveness. Leaders are accountable for their decisions, actions, and the well-being of those they lead. They set the tone for accountability within their teams and organizations by modeling responsible behavior and holding themselves and others to high standards.

4. Consequences and Learning: Accountability involves accepting the consequences of one's actions, whether positive or negative. It also includes learning from mistakes, identifying areas for improvement, and taking corrective action to prevent recurrence in the future.

5. Organizational Culture: Creating a culture of accountability within organizations is critical for promoting integrity, performance, and ethical behavior. This involves establishing clear expectations, communication channels, and systems for feedback, evaluation, and accountability.

6. Legal and Regulatory Compliance: In addition to ethical considerations, accountability may also involve compliance with legal and regulatory requirements. Organizations and individuals are accountable for adhering to laws, regulations, and industry standards relevant to their activities.

Overall, the "Law of Accountability" underscores the importance of integrity, responsibility, and transparency in personal and organizational conduct. It highlights the need for individuals and institutions to uphold ethical standards, take ownership of their actions, and work towards positive outcomes for themselves and society.

Chapter 28: Law of Artificial Intelligence

"AI is a tool. The choice of how it gets deployed is ours"

The "Law of Artificial Intelligence" is a recognition that we live in a world managed by technology and can be used as a tool for quick advancement. However, there are several principles, guidelines, and ethical frameworks that are often associated with the development and use of artificial intelligence (AI). These principles aim to ensure that AI systems are developed and deployed in a responsible, ethical, and beneficial manner.

Some common themes include:

1. Ethical AI: This principle emphasizes the importance of developing AI systems that align with ethical values such as fairness, transparency, accountability, and respect for human rights. Ethical AI frameworks often involve considering the potential societal impacts of AI technologies and ensuring that they benefit individuals and communities.

2. Human-Centered AI: Human-centered AI prioritizes the well-being and interests of humans in the design and deployment of AI systems. It involves considering human values, needs, and preferences throughout the development process and designing AI technologies that augment human capabilities and enhance quality of life.

3. Transparency and Explainability: AI systems should be transparent and explainable, meaning that their decisions and actions should be understandable and interpretable by humans. This principle is essential for building trust in AI technologies and enabling users to understand how AI systems work and why they make certain decisions.

4. Accountability and Responsibility: Developers and deployers of AI systems should be accountable for the outcomes and impacts of their technologies. This principle involves taking responsibility for addressing any negative consequences or biases that may arise from AI systems and ensuring that appropriate measures are in place to mitigate risks.

5. Bias and Fairness: AI systems should be designed and deployed in a way that mitigates biases and promotes fairness and equity. This principle involves identifying and addressing biases in training data, algorithms, and decision-making processes to ensure that AI systems do not discriminate against individuals or groups based on factors such as race, gender, or socioeconomic status.

These principles, along with others, contribute to shaping the responsible development, deployment, and governance of AI technologies. While there may not be a single "law" of artificial intelligence, these principles serve as important guidelines for ensuring that AI systems contribute positively to society while minimizing potential risks and harms.

Chapter 29: Law of Prestige

"Cultivate an aura of prestige and exclusivity to command admiration and loyalty."

The law of prestige suggests cultivating an aura of prestige and exclusivity to command admiration and loyalty. By positioning yourself or your brand as exclusive and desirable, you can create a sense of allure and reverence that attracts others and fosters loyalty. This involves leveraging quality, rarity, and exclusivity to elevate your status and differentiate yourself from competitors, ultimately enhancing your influence and impact.

The "Law of Prestige" is applicable in the early stages of development for any individual or organization. Below is a breakdown of the value of prestige:

1. Social Influence: In social psychology, prestige refers to the status, respect, or admiration that individuals or groups earn based on their achievements, expertise, or reputation. The law of prestige suggests that individuals or entities with high prestige may wield greater influence or authority in social interactions.

2. Leadership and Authority: Prestige can play a significant role in leadership and authority. Leaders who are perceived as prestigious, whether due to their expertise, accomplishments, or charisma, may have a greater ability to influence and inspire others.

3. Brand Image and Reputation: In marketing and branding, prestige often refers to the perceived value, exclusivity, and

desirability associated with certain brands or products. Companies may cultivate a sense of prestige through branding strategies, such as premium pricing, limited availability, or celebrity endorsements.

4. Cultural and Institutional Prestige: Prestige can also extend to cultural institutions, academic institutions, or professional organizations. Institutions with high prestige may attract top talent, resources, and recognition within their respective fields.

5. Ethical Considerations: While prestige can confer benefits and advantages, it's important to consider the ethical implications of pursuing or leveraging prestige. Individuals and organizations should strive to earn prestige through genuine achievements, ethical conduct, and contributions to society.

Overall, the "Law of Prestige" underscores the importance of reputation, credibility, and perceived value in influencing perceptions, behaviors, and outcomes in various domains of life. It highlights the role of prestige in shaping social hierarchies, leadership dynamics, consumer preferences, and institutional influence.

Chapter 30: Law of Rhythm

"If you accept the rhythms of life, you will never be disappointed. The blessing is coming"

The law of rhythm is a principle often associated with various esoteric and spiritual teachings. It suggests that everything in the universe moves in a rhythmic pattern, with cycles of ups and downs, expansions and contractions, or periods of activity and rest. This law implies that life operates in a cyclical manner rather than a linear one, and it governs various aspects of existence, including natural phenomena, human behavior, and even economic cycles.

Here's what the "Law of Rhythm" entails:

1. Natural Cycles: The Law of Rhythm acknowledges that everything in the universe follows cyclical patterns, including the rhythms of nature, the seasons, and the phases of the moon. These cycles are inherent in the fabric of existence and influence all aspects of life.

2. Ebb and Flow: Life is characterized by alternating periods of expansion and contraction, growth and decay, activity and rest. The Law of Rhythm teaches that these rhythms are natural and unavoidable, and that attempting to resist or disrupt them can lead to imbalance and disharmony.

3. Harmony and Balance: Living in harmony with the Law of Rhythm involves accepting and embracing the natural rhythms of life. It requires finding balance between activity and relaxation,

effort and surrender, and growth and reflection.

4. Personal Growth: The Law of Rhythm applies to personal growth and development as well. Individuals may experience periods of rapid progress followed by periods of stagnation or regression. Understanding and accepting these rhythms can help individuals navigate the ups and downs of their personal journeys.

5. Resilience: Recognizing the Law of Rhythm can cultivate resilience and adaptability. By understanding that challenging periods are temporary and part of a larger cycle, individuals can maintain hope and perspective during difficult times.

6. Spiritual Evolution: Some teachings suggest that the Law of Rhythm applies to spiritual evolution and consciousness expansion. According to these beliefs, individuals may experience cycles of spiritual growth, insight, and transformation as they progress on their spiritual path.

7. Flowing with Change: The Law of Rhythm teaches the importance of flowing with change rather than resisting it. By embracing the natural rhythms of life, individuals can cultivate greater peace, acceptance, and alignment with the unfolding of the universe.

Overall, the Law of Rhythm invites individuals to attune themselves to the natural cycles and rhythms of life, fostering a deeper connection to themselves, to others, and to the larger cosmos.

Chapter 31: Law of Persistence

"Persist in the pursuit of your goals, for resilience often triumphs over talent."

The law of persistence underscores the importance of persevering in the pursuit of your goals, as resilience often triumphs over talent alone. By maintaining a steadfast commitment and continuing to push forward despite obstacles or setbacks, you increase your chances of success. Persistence allows you to overcome challenges, learn from failures, and ultimately achieve your objectives through determination and resilience.

The "Law of Persistence" embodies the concept of perseverance and resilience in pursuing goals or overcoming obstacles. Here's a breakdown:

1. Continuous Effort: Persistence involves consistently applying effort and dedication toward achieving a desired outcome, even in the face of challenges or setbacks. It requires resilience, determination, and a willingness to keep going despite obstacles or failures.

2. Resilience in Adversity: The law of persistence acknowledges that setbacks and failures are a natural part of any endeavor. Instead of giving up when faced with difficulties, individuals who embody persistence view challenges as opportunities for growth and learning, and they continue to push forward toward their goals.

3. Long-Term Focus: Persistence often requires a long-term

perspective, as achieving significant goals may take time and sustained effort. It involves setting clear objectives, breaking them down into manageable steps, and staying focused on progress over time.

4. Adaptability and Flexibility: While persistence involves staying committed to a goal, it also requires adaptability and flexibility in response to changing circumstances. Individuals who are persistent are willing to adjust their strategies, seek feedback, and make necessary changes to overcome obstacles and achieve success.

5. Positive Mindset: Persistence is closely linked to a positive mindset and self-belief. Individuals who believe in their ability to overcome challenges and achieve their goals are more likely to persist in the face of adversity.

Overall, the "Law of Persistence" underscores the importance of perseverance, resilience, and determination in achieving success and overcoming obstacles. It emphasizes the power of persistence in turning setbacks into opportunities and realizing one's full potential.

Chapter 32: Law of Vulnerability

"Reveal vulnerability selectively to evoke empathy and forge deeper connections."

The law of vulnerability suggests revealing vulnerability selectively to evoke empathy and forge deeper connections with others. By sharing your vulnerabilities thoughtfully and authentically, you can create opportunities for empathy and understanding, strengthening bonds and fostering trust in relationships. However, it's important to exercise discernment in disclosing vulnerabilities, choosing appropriate contexts and trusted individuals with whom to share, to ensure that vulnerability enhances rather than undermines your connections.

The "Law of Vulnerability" is a strategic use of personal reality. While it can be intimidating at first, it is one of our most valuable assets as humans. Here is a breakdown of when and how:

1. Emotional Authenticity: Vulnerability involves the willingness to open oneself up emotionally, express one's true feelings, and share personal experiences with others. The law of vulnerability suggests that embracing vulnerability can foster deeper connections, trust, and intimacy in relationships.

2. Courage and Strength: Contrary to popular belief, vulnerability is not a sign of weakness but rather an indication of courage and strength. The law of vulnerability emphasizes that being vulnerable requires courage, as it involves stepping outside one's comfort zone and risking rejection or judgment from others.

3. Self-Acceptance and Growth: Embracing vulnerability is an essential part of self-acceptance and personal growth. It involves being honest with oneself about one's strengths, weaknesses, and limitations, and embracing all aspects of oneself with compassion and kindness.

4. Creativity and Innovation: Vulnerability can also fuel creativity and innovation. The law of vulnerability suggests that being open to new ideas, taking risks, and embracing failure as part of the creative process can lead to breakthroughs and transformative experiences.

5. Empathy and Connection: Vulnerability fosters empathy and connection with others by creating a space for authenticity and mutual understanding. When individuals are willing to show their vulnerability, it encourages others to do the same, leading to deeper, more meaningful relationships.

Overall, the "Law of Vulnerability" underscores the importance of embracing vulnerability as a path to authenticity, connection, and personal growth. It challenges the notion that vulnerability is a weakness and highlights its potential to cultivate courage, creativity, and compassion in individuals and communities.

Chapter 33: Law of Resourcefulness

"Adapt and thrive with limited resources through creativity and resourcefulness."

The law of resourcefulness emphasizes the ability to adapt and thrive with limited resources by harnessing creativity and ingenuity. By thinking outside the box, finding innovative solutions, and making the most of what's available, you can overcome constraints and achieve your goals effectively. Resourcefulness enables you to maximize the value of your resources, whether it's time, money, or materials, and navigate challenges with resilience and efficiency.

The "Law of Resourcefulness" embodies the concept of utilizing available resources creatively and effectively to achieve goals or solve problems. Here's a breakdown:

1. Creativity and Innovation: Resourcefulness involves thinking outside the box and finding inventive solutions to challenges. It requires creativity, adaptability, and a willingness to explore unconventional approaches to problem-solving.

2. Optimizing Resources: The law of resourcefulness emphasizes the importance of maximizing the use of available resources, whether they are financial, material, human, or intellectual. It involves leveraging existing assets and capabilities to their fullest potential.

3. Adaptability and Flexibility: Resourcefulness also requires

adaptability and flexibility in response to changing circumstances. Individuals who are resourceful are able to quickly assess situations, identify opportunities, and adapt their strategies accordingly.

4. Problem-Solving Skills: Resourcefulness is closely linked to effective problem-solving skills. It involves breaking down complex problems into manageable components, brainstorming creative solutions, and taking decisive action to address challenges.

5. Resilience and Persistence: Resourcefulness often goes hand in hand with resilience and persistence. When faced with obstacles or setbacks, resourceful individuals remain determined and resilient, seeking alternative paths forward rather than giving up easily.

6. Learning and Growth: Embracing resourcefulness fosters a mindset of continuous learning and growth. It encourages individuals to seek new knowledge, develop new skills, and expand their capabilities in order to better navigate future challenges.

Overall, the "Law of Resourcefulness" underscores the importance of creative thinking, adaptability, and perseverance in achieving success and overcoming obstacles. It highlights the power of leveraging available resources effectively to achieve desired outcomes and realize one's full potential.

Chapter 34: Law of Intimacy

"Intimacy is being seen and known as the person you truly are"

The law of influence suggests seeding ideas and beliefs subtly to shape opinions and behavior. By strategically planting thoughts and concepts in the minds of others through subtle persuasion and influence, you can gradually shape their perceptions and actions. This involves understanding the psychology of persuasion, crafting persuasive messages, and disseminating them strategically to gradually influence attitudes and behaviors over time.

The "Law of Intimacy" encompasses various aspects of close and authentic connections between individuals. Here's a breakdown:

1. Emotional Connection: Intimacy involves emotional closeness, vulnerability, and trust between individuals. It includes sharing feelings, thoughts, and experiences in a genuine and supportive manner.

2. Communication: Effective communication is essential for intimacy, as it allows individuals to express themselves honestly and openly, listen empathetically, and understand each other's perspectives.

3. Vulnerability: Intimacy requires being vulnerable and allowing oneself to be seen and accepted for who they truly are. It involves sharing fears, insecurities, and weaknesses with someone who is supportive and understanding.

4. Physical Intimacy: Physical intimacy can also be a part of intimate relationships, including gestures of affection, closeness, and sexual connection. However, physical intimacy is just one aspect of intimacy and does not necessarily define the depth of a relationship.

5. Trust and Respect: Intimacy is built on a foundation of trust and respect between individuals. It involves honoring boundaries, respecting privacy, and being reliable and dependable in the relationship.

6. Mutual Support and Understanding: Intimate relationships are characterized by mutual support, empathy, and understanding. Individuals in intimate relationships provide emotional support, offer encouragement, and show understanding during both good times and challenging times.

7. Commitment: Intimacy often involves a commitment to the relationship and a willingness to invest time, effort, and energy into nurturing and sustaining the connection over time.

Overall, the "Law of Intimacy" emphasizes the importance of deep, meaningful connections between individuals based on trust, vulnerability, and mutual understanding. It highlights the rewards of cultivating intimate relationships and the benefits of sharing one's life with others in an authentic and supportive manner.

Chapter 35: Law of Anticipation

"Anticipate and preempt your opponent's moves to maintain the upper hand."

The law of anticipation advises anticipating and preempting your opponent's moves to maintain the upper hand in any situation. By carefully studying your opponent's behavior, motivations, and patterns, you can predict their next moves and take proactive measures to counter or outmaneuver them. This involves staying several steps ahead, thinking strategically, and being prepared to adapt your tactics as the situation evolves, ultimately ensuring that you retain control and maintain a competitive advantage.

The "Law of Anticipation" is important for moving and thinking strategically. Here is a breakdown of applications:

1. Psychology: In psychology, the law of anticipation refers to the cognitive process of predicting or expecting future events based on past experiences, patterns, or information. Anticipation involves imagining possible outcomes, preparing for contingencies, and planning ahead to achieve desired goals.

2. Emotional Regulation: Anticipation plays a role in emotional regulation, as individuals may anticipate future events or situations that evoke certain emotions. This anticipation can influence how individuals prepare for and cope with emotional experiences.

3. Motivation and Goal Setting: Anticipation can be a powerful motivator for action and goal setting. The anticipation of achieving a desired outcome can drive individuals to take proactive

steps, set goals, and work towards realizing their aspirations.

4. Risk Management: In decision-making and risk management, anticipation involves anticipating potential risks, threats, or opportunities and taking proactive measures to mitigate risks or capitalize on opportunities before they arise.

5. Marketing and Consumer Behavior: Anticipation is also a key factor in marketing and consumer behavior. Businesses may use anticipation to create excitement, generate interest, and drive demand for products or services by teasing upcoming releases, promotions, or events.

6. Interpersonal Relationships: Anticipation can enhance interpersonal relationships by fostering anticipation for shared experiences, milestones, or moments of connection. Anticipating future interactions or events can strengthen bonds and create anticipation for future positive experiences together.

Overall, the "Law of Anticipation" underscores the importance of forward-thinking, planning, and preparation in various aspects of life. It highlights the role of anticipation in shaping behavior, emotions, and outcomes, and emphasizes the value of considering future possibilities when making decisions and navigating uncertainty.

Chapter 36: Law of Magnetism

"Cultivate magnetic charisma to draw others to your cause and vision."

The law of magnetism suggests cultivating magnetic charisma to attract others to your cause and vision. By embodying confidence, authenticity, and charm, you can captivate and inspire those around you, rallying them to support your goals and aspirations. This involves projecting a strong presence, connecting emotionally with others, and articulating your vision with conviction and passion, ultimately harnessing the power of charisma to lead and influence effectively.

The "Law of Magnetism" is a personal growth principal. It involves understanding one's strengths in order to rally others to your cause as demonstrated below:

1. Interpersonal Attraction: In social dynamics, the law of magnetism refers to the idea that certain individuals possess qualities or characteristics that attract others to them. Similar to how magnets attract metal objects, these individuals draw others to them through their charisma, confidence, or likability.

2. Leadership: In leadership, the law of magnetism suggests that effective leaders have a magnetic presence that inspires and motivates others to follow them. Their vision, passion, and ability to connect with people draw others to their cause or organization.

3. Personal Branding: In personal branding and marketing, the law of magnetism relates to the ability of individuals or brands to

attract an audience or customers through their unique identity, values, and messaging. A strong personal brand can create a magnetic pull that attracts followers, customers, or supporters.

4. Attraction in Relationships: The law of magnetism also applies to romantic relationships, where individuals may feel drawn to others who possess qualities or traits that complement or resonate with their own. This magnetic attraction can create chemistry, connection, and intimacy between partners.

5. Influence and Persuasion: The law of magnetism can also be associated with influence and persuasion. Individuals who exude confidence, authenticity, and charisma may have a magnetic effect on others, making them more persuasive and influential in their interactions.

Overall, the "Law of Magnetism" highlights the power of attraction and influence in various aspects of life. It emphasizes the importance of cultivating qualities such as authenticity, confidence, and charisma to create a magnetic presence that draws others to you and enhances your ability to lead, connect, and inspire.

Chapter 37: Law of Attraction

"Think the thought until you believe it, and once you believe it, it is."

The "Law of Attraction" is a concept often associated with the New Thought movement and popularized in the book "The Secret" by Rhonda Byrne. The reality of this principle is less rooted in the metaphysical or supernatural and more evident of the aligning of will and action.

Here's a breakdown of its key principles:

1. Like Attracts Like: The central idea of the Law of Attraction is that like attracts like. This means that the thoughts, beliefs, emotions, and intentions we put out into the universe attract similar energies or experiences back to us. In other words, positive thoughts attract positive outcomes, while negative thoughts attract negative outcomes.

2. Power of Visualization: Visualization is a key practice in applying the Law of Attraction. By visualizing and focusing on our desired outcomes with clarity, intensity, and emotion, we are believed to align our energy with those outcomes and attract them into our lives.

3. Affirmations: Affirmations are positive statements or declarations that we repeat to ourselves to reinforce positive beliefs and intentions. By affirming what we want to manifest in our lives, we align our thoughts and emotions with those desires and attract them into our reality.

4. Gratitude and Appreciation: Gratitude is considered a powerful tool for practicing the Law of Attraction. By expressing gratitude for what we already have and appreciating the blessings in our lives, we open ourselves up to receive more abundance and positive experiences.

5. Taking Inspired Action: While the Law of Attraction emphasizes the power of thoughts and beliefs in manifesting desires, it also emphasizes the importance of taking inspired action toward our goals. This involves being proactive, seizing opportunities, and aligning our actions with our intentions.

6. Letting Go of Resistance: Resistance, such as doubt, fear, or limiting beliefs, can block the flow of positive energy and hinder the manifestation process. Practicing the Law of Attraction involves letting go of resistance and trusting in the universe to deliver what is best for us.

7. Universal Energy: The Law of Attraction is based on the belief that everything in the universe is made up of energy, and that our thoughts and emotions are powerful energetic forces that shape our reality. By consciously directing our energy toward positive intentions, we can influence the outcomes we experience.

Overall, the Law of Attraction teaches that by focusing on positive thoughts, beliefs, and intentions, we can manifest our desires and create the life we want to live. While it has garnered both supporters and skeptics, many people find value in applying its principles to cultivate a more positive mindset and achieve their goals. It is most useful when viewed as a strategy for aligning thoughts, perspective, and action to move in accordance.

Chapter 38: Law of Power

"Mastering others is strength, mastering yourself is true power"

The "Law of Power" is a concept popularized by Robert Greene in his book "The 48 Laws of Power." It outlines principles and strategies for achieving and maintaining power in various aspects of life, including business, politics, and personal relationships.

Here's a breakdown of some of the key principles:

1. Never Outshine the Master: This law advises against overshadowing or appearing more capable than one's superiors, as it can breed envy and resentment. Instead, one should strive to make those in positions of power feel important and competent.

2. Conceal Your Intentions: This law suggests that revealing one's true intentions can make one vulnerable to manipulation or opposition. Instead, it advises maintaining a sense of mystery and strategically concealing one's motives to maintain an advantage.

3. Win Through Your Actions, Never Through Argument: Rather than engaging in fruitless arguments or debates, this law advises achieving victory through action and demonstration of competence. Actions speak louder than words, and success can often silence critics more effectively than argumentation.

4. Always Say Less Than Necessary: This law emphasizes the power of restraint in communication. By speaking less and listening more, one can avoid revealing too much information or

making unnecessary commitments. Silence can be a potent tool for maintaining an air of mystery and control.

5. Create a Sense of Urgency and Desperation: This law suggests that creating a sense of urgency and scarcity can motivate others to act in one's favor. By strategically creating a perception of limited time or opportunity, one can generate greater interest and commitment from others.

6. Use Absence to Increase Respect and Honor: This law highlights the power of scarcity and distance in enhancing one's perceived value and desirability. By strategically withdrawing or creating distance, one can increase anticipation and appreciation from others.

7. Crush Your Enemy Totally: This law advises against leaving room for potential retaliation or future threats. When confronting adversaries, it is often wiser to eliminate them completely rather than allowing them to regroup and pose a continued threat.

These are just a few examples of the laws outlined in "The 48 Laws of Power." While the book has garnered both praise and criticism for its Machiavellian approach to power dynamics, many readers find value in its insights for understanding human behavior and navigating complex social and professional environments.

Chapter 39: Law of Economic Warfare

"Money is a tool for the benefit of those who wield it. It is the destruction of those without"

The law of economic warfare refers to the use of economic tools and tactics to gain advantage over adversaries or achieve strategic objectives. It involves leveraging economic resources, policies, and measures to weaken opponents, bolster one's own position, or achieve specific goals.

The "Law of Economic Warfare" involves understanding finances in order to use them effectively to the practitioner's benefit. Here is a breakdown:

1. Tools and Tactics: Economic warfare encompasses a wide range of tools and tactics, including trade sanctions, tariffs, embargoes, financial sanctions, currency manipulation, cyber attacks, and economic espionage. These measures can target key industries, infrastructure, or individuals to exert pressure or influence on adversaries.

2. Goals and Objectives: The goals of economic warfare can vary depending on the geopolitical context and strategic objectives. It may include weakening the economy of a rival nation, disrupting supply chains, undermining political stability, coercing behavior change, or gaining leverage in negotiations or conflicts.

3. International Law and Ethics: While economic warfare can be a

powerful tool for achieving strategic goals, it also raises ethical and legal considerations. International law governs the use of economic sanctions and other economic measures, and their implementation must adhere to principles of proportionality, non-discrimination, and respect for human rights.

4. Impacts and Consequences: Economic warfare can have far-reaching impacts on both targeted nations and the global economy. It can disrupt trade flows, destabilize financial markets, exacerbate economic inequalities, and harm innocent civilians. As such, the use of economic warfare requires careful consideration of its potential consequences.

5. Countermeasures and Resilience: Nations targeted by economic warfare often employ countermeasures to mitigate its impact and build resilience. This may involve diversifying trade partners, developing domestic industries, strengthening economic alliances, and investing in technological innovation and infrastructure.

Overall, the "Law of Economic Warfare" underscores the strategic importance of economic tools and tactics in modern conflicts and geopolitical competition. It highlights the complex interplay between economics, politics, and security and emphasizes the need for careful consideration of the ethical, legal, and humanitarian implications of economic warfare measures.

Chapter 40: Law of Communication

"Communication is the solvent of all problems and is the foundation for personal development"

The law of communication refers to the importance of using clear language to move towards a common vision, goal, or objective. Clear communication of an organization's direction helps align everyone toward common goals and fosters a sense of purpose. The effectiveness of language used is evident in the outcomes of those interpreting the message.

The "Law of Communication" is a fundamental aspect of human interaction, and there are several principles and guidelines that govern effective communication:

1. Clarity: Effective communication requires clarity in conveying messages. This involves expressing ideas, thoughts, and information in a clear, concise, and easily understandable manner to ensure that the intended message is accurately received by the audience.

2. Active Listening: Communication is a two-way process that involves not only speaking but also listening actively to others. Active listening involves paying attention to verbal and non-verbal cues, seeking clarification when necessary, and empathizing with the speaker's perspective.

3. Non-Verbal Communication: Non-verbal cues such as body language, facial expressions, gestures, and tone of voice play a significant role in communication. The law of communication emphasizes the importance of non-verbal communication in conveying emotions, intentions, and attitudes.

4. Empathy and Understanding: Effective communication requires empathy and understanding of the audience's perspectives, emotions, and needs. Empathetic communication involves acknowledging others' feelings, validating their experiences, and showing respect and compassion.

5. Feedback and Confirmation: Communication is enhanced by providing and receiving feedback to ensure mutual understanding and clarity. The law of communication encourages seeking feedback, asking questions, and confirming understanding to prevent misunderstandings and promote effective dialogue.

6. Adaptability: Effective communicators are adaptable and able to adjust their communication style and approach based on the needs, preferences, and cultural backgrounds of the audience. Flexibility in communication allows for better rapport-building and connection with others.

7. Transparency and Honesty: Trust is essential for effective communication. The law of communication emphasizes the importance of transparency, honesty, and integrity in conveying information. Being truthful and authentic fosters trust and credibility in communication.

8. Conflict Resolution: Communication plays a crucial role in resolving conflicts and addressing disagreements constructively.

Effective communication techniques such as active listening, empathy, and assertiveness can help de-escalate conflicts and find mutually acceptable solutions.

Overall, the "Law of Communication" highlights the principles and strategies for fostering clear, empathetic, and respectful communication in various interpersonal, professional, and social contexts. It emphasizes the importance of mutual understanding, trust, and authenticity in building positive relationships and achieving successful outcomes through communication.

Chapter 41: Law of Spiritual Warfare

"The truth is that there is an enemy and he's out to destroy us"

The "Law of Spiritual Warfare" is a concept often associated with religious or spiritual beliefs and practices, particularly within Christianity and other faith traditions. It refers to the spiritual struggle or battle between good and evil, and the efforts to overcome spiritual obstacles or challenges. In order to understand the ebb and flow of the world, we must be able to recognize the external forces at play and acknowledge them.

Though there are many explanations for physical realities, there are cases in which only a spiritual explanation will suffice. The ability to assent to a higher power allows us the freedom to rest in a plan we may not currently be understanding. Here's a breakdown:

1. Spiritual Realm: The law of spiritual warfare recognizes the existence of a spiritual realm beyond the physical world, where supernatural forces, including angels and demons, are believed to be active. It acknowledges the ongoing spiritual battle between forces of light and darkness.

2. Good vs. Evil: Spiritual warfare involves the conflict between forces of good, which may include God, angels, and divine beings, and forces of evil, such as Satan, demons, and malevolent spirits. This battle is often depicted metaphorically as a struggle between

righteousness and sin, truth and deception, or light and darkness.

3. Weapons and Strategies: In spiritual warfare, individuals may employ various weapons and strategies to combat spiritual forces of evil and overcome spiritual obstacles. These may include prayer, meditation, fasting, scripture study, worship, and spiritual disciplines aimed at strengthening one's faith and connection with the divine.

4. Armor of God: The concept of the "Armor of God," mentioned in the Bible (Ephesians 6:10-18), is often invoked in spiritual warfare. It refers to spiritual armor that believers are encouraged to put on to protect themselves from spiritual attacks and to stand firm against the schemes of the devil.

5. Victory and Redemption: The ultimate goal of spiritual warfare is victory over evil and the restoration of spiritual wholeness and harmony. It involves resisting temptation, overcoming spiritual strongholds, and experiencing spiritual transformation and redemption through faith, grace, and divine intervention.

6. Community and Support: Spiritual warfare is often viewed as a communal endeavor, with believers supporting and praying for one another in their spiritual battles. Community and fellowship provide strength, encouragement, and accountability in the face of spiritual challenges.

7. Discernment and Discipleship: Discernment is essential in spiritual warfare, as individuals are called to discern the sources of spiritual influences and discern between truth and deception. Discipleship involves growing in spiritual maturity, wisdom, and discernment through ongoing spiritual practices and guidance.

Overall, the law of spiritual warfare underscores the belief in a spiritual battle between good and evil and the importance of spiritual preparedness, discernment, and reliance on divine power to overcome spiritual challenges and obstacles. It emphasizes the role of faith, prayer, and spiritual disciplines in maintaining spiritual strength and victory in the face of spiritual warfare. While it acknowledges forces beyond our knowledge or reason, it encourages us to take action and draw from a source of higher power. Recognizing we are not fully in charge of our lives or the outcomes we face is important for navigating struggles when they surface.

Chapter 42: Law of Consent

"Permission is the key to earning the respect of those granting it"

The law of consent is a clear and voluntary agreement or permission given by an individual to engage in a specific activity, action, or interaction. It involves the acknowledgment and acceptance of boundaries, desires, and preferences by all parties involved. It is the foundation by which all agreements are based.

The "Law of Consent" refers to the legal principle that governs the voluntary agreement between parties to engage in a particular activity or transaction. Here's a breakdown:

1. Voluntary Agreement: Consent is the voluntary and informed agreement between parties to engage in a specific action or activity. It requires that individuals have the capacity and understanding to make a decision freely, without coercion, manipulation, or deception.

2. Legal Capacity: For consent to be valid, individuals must have the legal capacity to give consent. This means they must be of legal age, mentally competent, and not under the influence of drugs, alcohol, or coercion that impairs their ability to make informed decisions.

3. Informed Consent: Informed consent requires that individuals have sufficient information about the nature, purpose, risks, and consequences of the activity or transaction before giving consent. This allows individuals to make informed decisions based on an

understanding of the relevant facts.

4. Specificity: Consent must be specific to the particular activity or transaction in question. General consent does not necessarily apply to all situations and may be limited in scope or duration based on the circumstances.

5. Revocability: Consent is generally revocable, meaning that individuals have the right to withdraw or revoke their consent at any time, provided they have the capacity to do so. However, revocation of consent may have legal consequences depending on the nature of the agreement or activity.

6. Consent in Different Contexts: Consent plays a crucial role in various legal contexts, including contracts, medical treatment, sexual relationships, research participation, and more. Each context may have specific requirements and standards for obtaining valid consent.

7. Importance in Ethics and Human Rights: Consent is fundamental to ethical principles of autonomy, respect for individuals' rights, and dignity. It is also enshrined in human rights frameworks, such as the right to bodily integrity and self-determination.

Overall, the law of consent emphasizes the importance of respecting individuals' autonomy, agency, and decision-making capacity in all aspects of life. It serves as a cornerstone of ethical conduct, legal agreements, and human rights protection, ensuring that individuals have the freedom to make choices that affect their lives.

Chapter 43: Law of Sacrifice

"Make strategic sacrifices to gain leverage and advance your agenda."

The law of sacrifice advises making strategic sacrifices to gain leverage and advance your agenda. By relinquishing certain assets, resources, or positions strategically, you can create opportunities for negotiation, reciprocity, or strategic positioning that ultimately serve your larger objectives. This involves weighing the costs and benefits of each sacrifice carefully, ensuring that the sacrifices made are calculated and strategic, leading to greater gains or advantages in the long run.

Here's a deeper explanation of the concept:

1.Value Exchange: The Law of Sacrifice involves a fundamental exchange of value. It implies that in order to gain or achieve something meaningful, one must be prepared to relinquish or sacrifice something else in return. This sacrifice can take many forms, such as time, effort, resources, comfort, or even personal desires.

2.Prioritization: Sacrifice often entails prioritizing long-term goals or values over short-term gratification or convenience. It requires individuals to make choices and allocate their resources in a way that aligns with their highest priorities and aspirations.

3.Commitment and Dedication: Embracing the Law of Sacrifice requires commitment and dedication to a cause or goal. It involves a willingness to endure temporary discomfort or setbacks in pursuit of something greater, knowing that the sacrifices made are investments in one's future success or fulfillment.

4.Personal Growth and Development: Sacrifice is often associated with personal growth and development. By letting go of what is familiar or comfortable, individuals can challenge themselves, expand their capabilities, and evolve into their best selves. Sacrifice can foster resilience, perseverance, and character development.

5.Alignment with Values: Sacrifice should be aligned with one's core values, beliefs, and aspirations. It involves consciously choosing what is most important and meaningful, and being willing to make sacrifices that are in harmony with one's values and vision for life.

6.Balancing Sacrifice and Self-Care: While sacrifice can be a powerful tool for growth and achievement, it's important to strike a balance between self-sacrifice and self-care. Sacrificing too much without attending to one's own well-being can lead to burnout, resentment, or imbalance. It's essential to prioritize self-care and ensure that sacrifices are sustainable and in alignment with overall health and well-being.

Overall, the Law of Sacrifice underscores the principle that meaningful achievements often require sacrifice and effort. By embracing sacrifice consciously and purposefully, individuals can pursue their highest aspirations, achieve personal growth, and create lives of purpose and fulfillment.

Chapter 44: Law of Financial Freedom

"Financial freedom is freedom from fear."

The law of financial freedom is a wealth based initiative. Only those who are free from the slavery of working daily to feed their families or other dependents are truly capable of living life as it was intended. To be financially free is to have endless opportunity for development, expansion, and domination.

The "Law of Financial Freedom" is a concept that encompasses principles and strategies aimed at achieving financial independence and security. Here's what it entails:

1. Definition: Financial freedom refers to the ability to live comfortably and pursue your desired lifestyle without being constrained by financial limitations. It involves having sufficient income and resources to cover expenses, achieve financial goals, and enjoy a fulfilling life.

2. Income Diversification: One key principle of financial freedom is diversifying sources of income. This may include earning from multiple streams such as salary, investments, passive income (e.g., rental properties, dividends), and entrepreneurial ventures.

3. Budgeting and Saving: Financial freedom often requires disciplined budgeting and saving habits. This involves living within your means, prioritizing savings and investments, and avoiding

unnecessary expenses or debt.

4. Debt Management: Managing debt is essential for achieving financial freedom. This may involve paying off high-interest debt, such as credit card debt, and using debt strategically for investments that generate positive returns.

5. Investing: Investing plays a crucial role in building wealth and achieving financial freedom. This may include investing in stocks, bonds, real estate, retirement accounts, and other assets that have the potential to grow over time and generate passive income.

6. Financial Planning: Developing a comprehensive financial plan is essential for achieving financial freedom. This involves setting clear financial goals, creating a budget, establishing an emergency fund, and planning for major expenses such as retirement, education, and healthcare.

7. Risk Management: Assessing and managing risks is important for maintaining financial stability and security. This may involve having insurance coverage for health, life, property, and disability, as well as diversifying investments to mitigate investment risk.

8. Lifestyle Choices: Lifestyle choices can significantly impact financial freedom. This includes making conscious decisions about spending, prioritizing experiences over material possessions, and avoiding lifestyle inflation that can erode wealth over time.

9. Continuous Learning and Adaptation: Achieving financial freedom requires ongoing learning, adaptation, and adjustment. Keeping abreast of financial trends, market conditions, and personal finance strategies allows individuals to make informed

decisions and optimize their financial situation.

Overall, the Law of Financial Freedom emphasizes the importance of financial literacy, discipline, and strategic planning in achieving independence, security, and peace of mind in one's financial life. Individuals and organizations that are capable of achieving financial freedom are capable of acquiring more responsibility and assets. Financial freedom is one of the key principles to developing an autonomous empire.

Chapter 45: Law of Gratitude

"Those who are not grateful soon begin to complain of everything"

The law of gratitude is a principal rooted in recognition of the things that have gone right so as to continue to develop more opportunities for success. Organizations and individuals capable of consistently recognizing the small wins in their life will typically see larger wins more often.

The "Law of Gratitude" emphasizes the importance of acknowledging and appreciating the positive aspects of life. Here's what it entails:

1. Recognition: The Law of Gratitude involves recognizing and acknowledging the good things, experiences, and people in our lives, no matter how small or seemingly insignificant they may be.

2. Appreciation: Gratitude goes beyond recognition; it involves feeling and expressing appreciation for the blessings and opportunities we have been given. It involves taking the time to reflect on the things that bring us joy, fulfillment, and meaning.

3. Mindfulness: Practicing gratitude requires being present and mindful of the present moment, noticing and savoring the positive aspects of life rather than dwelling on what is lacking or negative.

4. Positive Outlook: Cultivating an attitude of gratitude can lead to a more positive outlook on life. It can help shift our focus away from negativity and pessimism, fostering resilience and emotional

well-being.

5. Connection: Gratitude fosters a sense of connection with others. When we express gratitude, we acknowledge the contributions and kindnesses of others, strengthening our relationships and building a sense of community.

6. Generosity: Gratitude often leads to a desire to give back and pay it forward. When we feel grateful for what we have received, we may be more inclined to help others and make a positive difference in their lives.

7. Health Benefits: Research has shown that practicing gratitude is associated with numerous health benefits, including improved mental health, reduced stress, greater resilience, and enhanced overall well-being.

In essence, the Law of Gratitude encourages us to focus on the positive aspects of life, cultivate a sense of appreciation and abundance, and foster connections with others. By practicing gratitude regularly, we can experience greater happiness, fulfillment, and satisfaction in our lives.

Chapter 46: Law of Network

"You can have anything you want in life if you help enough people get what they want"

The law of network is crucial to the success of any individual or organization. Developing a network of individuals or like minded supporters allows for expansion and reach. Without a highly developed network, the individual is an island with no additional resources beyond their reach.

The "Law of Network" refers to principles and concepts related to network theory, social networks, or information networks. Here are some key aspects:

1. Connectivity: The Law of Network emphasizes the importance of connections and relationships between nodes or entities within a network. It highlights that the structure and strength of connections influence the overall functioning and resilience of the network.

2. Network Effects: This principle suggests that the value of a network increases as more users or nodes join it. Network effects can lead to exponential growth, increased interaction, and enhanced utility for participants.

3. Small World Phenomenon: The Law of Network may also refer to the "small world" phenomenon, which posits that any two individuals in a social network are connected by a relatively small number of intermediaries. This idea has been popularized by the concept of "six degrees of separation."

4. Scale-Free Networks: In some cases, networks exhibit a scale-free structure, characterized by a few highly connected nodes (hubs) and many less-connected nodes. The Law of Network may involve understanding the distribution of connections and the role of hubs in influencing network dynamics.

5. Resilience and Robustness: Networks can display resilience and robustness in the face of disruptions or attacks. The Law of Network involves understanding how network structure, redundancy, and adaptability contribute to resilience against failures or malicious actions.

6. Information Flow: Networks facilitate the flow of information, resources, or influence between nodes. The Law of Network may involve studying patterns of information diffusion, propagation of trends, or contagion of behaviors within networks.

7. Community and Clustering: Networks often exhibit clustering or community structure, where nodes form tightly interconnected groups or clusters. The Law of Network involves understanding how these community structures influence network dynamics, information diffusion, and social interactions.

Overall, the Law of Network encompasses various principles and phenomena related to the structure, function, and dynamics of networks in different domains, including social, biological, technological, and information networks. Understanding these principles can provide insights into the behavior of complex systems and facilitate the design and management of networks for optimal performance and resilience.

Chapter 47: Law of Deprivation

"If you can survive with less, you will learn to thrive when more comes"

The law of deprivation encompasses the notion that those who are without a resource will typically find, by any means, the solution to their problem. Deprivation can also be a personal choice so as not to be distracted by the allure of frivolous things. Either way, it is important to recognize that deprivation is a tool that not only drives the value of an object or desire, but can also be a key motivation when used with purpose.

The "Law of Deprivation" can be interpreted in various contexts as listed below:

1. Psychological Perspective: In psychology, the law of deprivation refers to the theory that individuals or groups that perceive themselves as deprived of resources, opportunities, or status may be more likely to engage in behaviors aimed at obtaining what they feel they lack. This theory suggests that feelings of deprivation can drive motivation and behavior.

2. Economic Theory: In economics, the law of deprivation may refer to the idea that scarcity or deprivation of resources can drive demand and influence economic behavior. Individuals or societies experiencing deprivation may prioritize the acquisition of goods or services that they perceive as essential or valuable.

3. Conflict and Instability: The law of deprivation may also be relevant in understanding conflicts and social unrest. Feelings of deprivation, whether real or perceived, can contribute to social tensions, grievances, and protests as individuals or groups seek to address their unmet needs or demands.

Overall, the concept of the law of deprivation underscores the importance of recognizing the difference between intentional withholding of resources and starvation. While there is a proper way to create scarcity and drive up value and motivation, the ethical practice will ensure that no one is deprived of dignity, worth, or basic necessities in the process. Just as overstocking an item can be detrimental to value, going too far in creating scarcity can lead to ruin if there is not a continuous opportunity for more of what is desired.

Chapter 48: Law of Prudence

"He who is prudent and lies in wait for an enemy who is not, will be victorious"

The law of prudence advises exercising caution and discretion in your dealings to minimize risk and maximize reward. By carefully assessing the potential risks and rewards of each decision or action, you can make informed choices that enhance your chances of success while mitigating potential pitfalls. This involves considering various factors such as potential consequences, uncertainties, and alternative options, and taking calculated steps to achieve your objectives in a way that prioritizes long-term sustainability and success.

The "Law of Prudence" refers to the principle of acting with caution, foresight, and careful consideration of potential consequences. It's a foundational concept in various fields, including law, finance, and ethics as listed below:

1. In legal contexts, prudence suggests that individuals or entities should exercise reasonable care and diligence in their actions to avoid harm or legal liability. This involves assessing risks, making informed decisions, and taking appropriate precautions.

2. In finance, the law of prudence guides investors and financial professionals to make decisions that prioritize long-term stability and risk management over short-term gains. It involves conducting thorough research, diversifying investments, and avoiding unnecessary risks.

3. Ethically, prudence encourages individuals to consider the impact of their actions on themselves and others, striving to act in ways that promote well-being and minimize harm.

Overall, the law of prudence emphasizes the importance of thoughtful, responsible behavior in various aspects of life. It is wise to think twice and act once when facing difficult decisions. Leadership often requires foresight in navigating situations, relationships, and finances. Prudence is a principal that allows individuals and organizations to continuously consider external and internal factors before making decisions that could alter their potential future.

Chapter 49: Law of Independence

"Becoming independent is a test of personal resilience and innovation"

The law of independence focuses on creating unique opportunities. In order to be be different, an individual or organization must not be like anyone else. Independence is a requirement of all pioneers in innovation. Without unique thoughts, designs, and movements, the world would be without innovation. While this idea may sound contradictory to networking and relationship building, it is simply the foundation that one must have in order to avoid becoming a follower.

The "Law of Independence" can be applied in social, political, or philosophical contexts. For example:

 1. Independence of Thought: This refers to the ability and freedom of individuals to form their own opinions, beliefs, and judgments without undue influence or coercion from external sources. It encompasses critical thinking, intellectual autonomy, and the courage to challenge prevailing norms or ideologies.

 2. Political Independence: This refers to the autonomy and sovereignty of nations or regions from external control or interference. It encompasses concepts such as national self-determination, independence movements, and the establishment of democratic governance systems free from colonial or authoritarian rule.

c3. Economic Independence: This refers to the ability of individuals, communities, or nations to sustain themselves economically without relying excessively on external aid or resources. It involves promoting self-sufficiency, entrepreneurship, and equitable economic development.

4. Personal Independence: This refers to individual autonomy and self-reliance in decision-making, lifestyle choices, and actions. It encompasses concepts such as personal freedom, agency, and the ability to pursue one's goals and aspirations without undue constraints or dependencies.

5. Interdependence: While independence is important, it is also recognized that individuals, communities, and nations are interconnected and interdependent in various ways. The concept of interdependence emphasizes the importance of cooperation, collaboration, and mutual support in addressing shared challenges and achieving common goals.

These interpretations highlight different aspects of independence and its significance in various domains of human life and society. While the concept of independence may manifest differently in different contexts, it often represents a fundamental value associated with freedom, autonomy, and self-determination.

Chapter 50: Law of Existence

"The greatest gift in the world is your next breath. Learn to appreciate the small things"

The "law of existence" is a principle derived from mindfulness practices. It essentially advocates for focusing one's attention on the present moment rather than dwelling on the past or worrying about the future. This principle is often associated with various mental health practices and philosophies, including mindfulness meditation and certain schools of thought in psychology and spirituality.

The "Law of Existence" can be applied to various disciplines in your life as outline below:

1.Awareness: Existence involves cultivating a heightened awareness of one's thoughts, emotions, bodily sensations, and surroundings. This awareness is nonjudgmental and accepting, allowing individuals to observe their experiences without getting caught up in them.

2.Present Moment Focus: Existence emphasizes focusing attention on the present moment, rather than dwelling on the past or worrying about the future. By staying grounded in the here and now, individuals can reduce stress and anxiety associated with ruminating on past events or anticipating future challenges.

3.Acceptance: Existence encourages acceptance of one's experiences, whether they are pleasant, unpleasant, or neutral. Instead of trying to change or resist reality, individuals are encouraged to acknowledge their thoughts and feelings without judgment. This acceptance fosters inner peace and emotional resilience.

4.Non-Reactivity: Existence involves cultivating a non-reactive stance towards internal and external stimuli. Rather than impulsively reacting to thoughts, emotions, or external events, individuals learn to respond thoughtfully and skillfully. This increased self-awareness can lead to healthier decision-making and improved interpersonal relationships.

5.Equanimity: Practicing existence promotes a sense of equanimity or balance in the face of life's ups and downs. By developing a stable and compassionate attitude towards oneself and others, individuals can navigate challenges with greater resilience and emotional stability.

Overall, the law existence is a practice that involves training the mind to be fully present, open, and accepting of one's experiences. Through regular practice, individuals can cultivate greater self-awareness, inner peace, and overall well-being. By doing so, it's believed that people can experience greater clarity, reduce stress, and enhance their overall well-being. It is important to remember that navigating diverse situations can only be handled when the individual is in a healthy space and fully available to respond to the situations that arise on daily basis.

Conclusion:

In the ever-shifting landscape of power and influence, mastery of the fifty laws outlined in "The Code of Influence" is the key to success. By understanding and applying these principles with wisdom and integrity, you can navigate the complexities of human interaction, shape your destiny, and leave a lasting legacy in the annals of history.

Other Works by Luciano Layne

13 Letters to My Children

S.A.M.Y.R.A.

Follow on Instagram

@iamlucianolayne